Published by Ladybird Books Ltd
A Penguin Company
Penguin Books Ltd, 80 Strand, London, WC2R 0RL, England
Penguin Books Australia Ltd, Camberwell, Victoria, Australia
Penguin Group (NZ), cnr Airborne and Rosedale Roads, Albany, Auckland 1310, New Zealand

3 5 7 9 10 8 6 4 2

Ladybird and the device of a ladybird are trademarks of Ladybird Books Ltd

Manufactured in Italy

www.ladybird.co.uk

Disney PRESENTS A PIXAR FILM

THE INCREDIBLES
MEET THE GIRLS

Ladybird

THE INCREDIBLES – MEET THE GIRLS

Elastigirl

Elastigirl has incredible stretching powers. In the golden age of heroes, she was fast becoming one of the world's top Supers. Her secret identity is Helen Parr, a seemingly ordinary housewife and mother of three children.

Violet

Violet is Helen's teenage Super daughter. She soon realises that being Super is in her blood.

Edna Mode

Edna Mode is the fashion designer to the world's top supermodels (and the Supers). She really misses the glory days of the Supers, which is why she's very pleased when Bob comes for a visit. Perhaps he comes with a challenge?

Mirage

For every villain there is an assistant. In the case of Syndrome, it is the very glamorous and highly mysterious Mirage.

HELEN PARR...
wife, mother

To her friends and neighbours, Helen Parr is just like them – an ordinary wife and mother to three children.

But Helen's family is far from ordinary. They just happen to be Supers – heroes with amazing powers. They are the Incredibles.

Helen's Super stretching ability helps her to get things done around the home in Super quick time, and it helps keep her children under control. Helen is very careful to make sure her neighbours don't see just how "flexible" she really is!

Helen has strong instincts. She senses Bob is hiding something. A few phone calls confirm what she already suspects – her husband is doing hero work behind her back.

Though Helen tries hard to lead a normal life, she literally springs into action when her family is put in danger.

ELASTIGIRL... *heroine returns*

In her former life as a Super, Helen was Elastigirl. She was able to stretch herself to catch a criminal from a whole street away. Bad guys had no chance against this high-kicking Super.

When she suspects her husband is in trouble, Helen puts on the new Super suit that Edna has made for her, and hurries to her husband. Her new suit has been designed with her special power in mind. It's made of super-stretch material, so it can stretch as far as she can.

Elastigirl even stretches herself into the shape of a boat, after her plane crashes into the sea.

LEAVE THE SAVING OF THE WORLD TO THE MEN? I DON'T THINK SO.

SURE, I HAVE A SECRET IDENTITY. WHO'D WANT TO GO SHOPPING AS ELASTIGIRL? YOU KNOW WHAT I MEAN?

ELASTIGIRL'S JOKES

Why shouldn't you play board games with Elastigirl?
She tends to stretch the rules.

What is Elastigirl's favourite kind of pop group?
Elastic bands!

VIOLET: Mom, can you lend me ten dollars?
ELASTIGIRL: Oh, I think I can stretch to that...

What kind of car would Elastigirl like to drive?
A stretch-limo!

What do you call Elastigirl with sunburn?
Mrs Pinkredible.

Is Elastigirl stubborn and pig-headed?
No, she really is very flexible.

VIOLET...
shy girl

Violet Parr – a normal teenage girl? Always hiding behind her hair, she's shy, awkward and just wants to blend in. She's frustrated that her family can't just be 'normal'.

To make matters worse, her annoying younger brother Dash, keeps teasing her about her crush on Tony Rydinger!

But, being an Incredible means that she is no ordinary girl. For a shy teenager, she has the perfect special power: Violet can make herself invisible. It's ideal for a girl who desperately wants to hide.

She can also throw force fields. When Dash slaps her on the back of the head, she throws a force field in his path as he runs at high speed - ouch!!!

NORMAL? WHAT DOES ANYONE IN THIS FAMILY KNOW ABOUT BEING NORMAL?

SOMETIMES I JUST WANT TO DISAPPEAR.

VIOLET...
Super girl

Violet has always wanted to hide her powers, but when the villain Syndrome puts her family in danger, she realises that she has more power than she thought.

At first Violet is not very confident using her powers, but she soon realises she's a true Super. She learns she can generate large powerful force fields, and that once inside, no one can get to her – not even Syndrome.

She even uses her force field to escape Syndrome's immobi-rays. Then she frees her entire family!

Violet's Super suit is made from fabric that disappears when she does!

The whole adventure changes Violet. The exciting rescue makes Violet a **little** less shy, and the boys? Well they seem to be taking a **lot** more notice of her!

VIOLET'S JOKES

What did Violet's boyfriend do when she went invisible?
Stopped seeing her.

Why was Dash missing Violet so much?
He hadn't seen much of her lately!

What does Violet paint her fingertips with?
Nail vanish.

What kind of pen does Violet use?
One with invisible ink!

What position does Violet play in cricket?
She's a force-fielder.

MIRAGE...
villain's assistant

Every devious villain needs a trusty assistant. Mirage is Syndrome's right-hand women. She is glamorous, mysterious and is totally in control of the smooth running of Syndrome's operation.

Mirage is responsible for finding and recruiting retired Supers for new missions. She tricks them into fighting the Omnidroid, leading to their certain death.

At first Mirage follows Frozone – she thinks he might be the next Super to fight the Omnidroid. But when she sees Mr Incredible she realises that he is the one that Syndrome has been waiting for.

THE SUPERS AREN'T GONE, MR INCREDIBLE. YOU'RE STILL HERE. YOU CAN STILL DO GREAT THINGS!

Mirage tells Mr Incredible she works for a top secret division of the government that designs and tests experimental technology. She tells him that a prototype robot is out of control and needs to be stopped.

MIRAGE...
change of heart

After Mr Incredible's first mission he wonders who Mirage is really working for. She tells him that her boss likes to remain anonymous. At dinner with Mirage, Mr Incredible learns that she is attracted to power just like her boss.

Later when Mr Incredible thinks he has lost his family forever, Mirage feels a prick of conscience. Syndrome does not value life and she realises that she has been working for the wrong side.

EDNA MODE...
fashionista

Edna Mode (known as E) is a brilliant and successful fashion designer. She made a name for herself designing outfits for the Supers in the old days.

Despite her international success, E would like nothing more than to see the return of the Supers, because she could make use of the latest technology in their outfits.

Designing for supermodels is not the same as designing for Supers.
"Supermodels... HAH! Nothing super about them. Spoiled, stupid little stick figures with poofy lips who think only about themselves – FEH! I used to design for Gods! Hmmm... But perhaps you come with a challenge, eh?"

She has one very important rule when designing new Super suits – **no capes**. To her, they are outdated. What's more, they're dangerous!

When Mr Incredible asks her to make him a new Super suit, she takes it on herself to make outfits for every other member of the Incredibles family too.

> NOTHING BUT AN OLD HOBO SUIT!

EDNA'S JOKES

How might you describe Edna Mode's glasses?
Specs-tacular.

Which is Edna's least favourite city?
Cape Town.

Why won't Edna Mode design Super cloaks?
She just can't cape!

Why doesn't Edna design Super suits with lots of buttons?
They are too hard to fashion.

EDNA'S WORDS OF WISDOM

THIS IS A HOBO SUIT, DARLING,
YOU CAN'T BE SEEN IN THIS.
I WON'T ALLOW IT. FIFTEEN YEARS AGO,
MAYBE. BUT NOW... FEH!

YOU ARE ELASTIGIRL! MY GOD,
PULL YOURSELF TOGETHER!
WHAT WILL YOU DO?
IS THIS A QUESTION?

I NEVER LOOK BACK, DARLING,
IT DISTRACTS FROM THE NOW.
YOU NEED A NEW SUIT. THAT MUCH
IS CERTAIN...

THIS PROJECT HAS COMPLETELY CONFISCATED MY LIFE, DARLING... CONSUMED ME AS ONLY HERO WORK CAN. MY BEST WORK I MUST ADMIT. SIMPLE. ELEGANT, YET BOLD. YOU WILL DIE.

YOU NEED A SUIT THAT'S BOLD, DYNAMIC!